A Kalmus Classic Edition

George Frideric

HANDEL

SIX ORGAN CONCERTOS
Opus 7

FOR ORGAN

K 02266

CONTENTS

VORWORT

Die günstige Aufnahme, die den ersten sechs Orgelkonzerten von Händel in der Übertragung des Herausgebers für Orgel allein zuteil wurde, hat den Verlag ermutigt, hier die Konzerte 7—12 (Händels op. 7, Nr. 1—6) folgen zu lassen. Die Grundsätze der Bearbeitung sind dieselben geblieben: der Orchesterpart ist in der Regel dem Hauptwerk der Orgel (HW), der Solopart dem Oberwerk (OW) zugeteilt. Die innerhalb eines Satzes mit ad libitum bezeichneten Stellen, die Händel, wenn er diese Konzerte selbst spielte, improvisatorisch weitergeführt hat, wurden vom Herausgeber ergänzt; wo ganze Sätze mit ad libitum bezeichnet sind, wurden sie aus anderen Werken Händels übernommen. Die Tempoangaben sind original, ebenso die groß gedruckten dynamischen Zeichen; Zusätze des Herausgebers sind durch kleineren Druck kenntlich gemacht.

Nach den ersten sechs, 1738 erschienenen Orgelkonzerten Händels, die sich sofort sowohl als Konzert- wie als Hausmusik großer Beliebtheit erfreuten, kamen schon 1739/40 sechs weitere heraus, die aber keine Originale, sondern Übertragungen aus den Concerti grossi darstellten. Es ist nicht sicher, ob Händel an dieser Ausgabe überhaupt beteiligt war. Erst nach seinem Tod, im Jahr 1760, erschienen als op. 7 wieder sechs originale Orgelkonzerte, die in der Zeit von 1740 bis 1751 entstanden waren. Im Einzelnen sei zu diesen Konzerten bemerkt:

Nr. 7 (op. 7, Nr. 1) nimmt insofern eine Ausnahmestellung unter Händels Orgelkonzerten ein, als hier ausdrücklich zwei Manuale und Pedal gefordert werden; hier wird auch eine Zungenstimme im Manual verlangt („Basson"). Händel hat es am 17. Februar 1740 vollendet; für welche Orgel es bestimmt war, ist nicht bekannt. Die beiden ersten Sätze haben die Form einer Chaconne. Hier muß der Wechsel von Hauptwerk und Oberwerk in der Registrierung besonders deutlich zum Ausdruck kommen.

Nr. 8 (op. 7 Nr. 2), vollendet am 5. Februar 1743 in London, steht in strahlendem A-dur und beginnt mit einer groß ausgeführten französischen Ouvertüre. Die Adagioüberleitung zwischen den beiden Allegrosätzen wurde aus einer Triosonate von Händel genommen.

Nr. 9 (op. 7, Nr. 3), in B-dur, wurde 1741 begonnen, aber erst am 4. Januar 1751 vollendet. Das Hauptthema des ersten Satzes klingt an das Halleluja aus dem Messias an. Für den Schlußsatz stellt Händel zwei Menuette zur Wahl. Zwischen dem ersten und zweiten Satz soll ein „Adagio e Fuga" improvisiert werden; sie wurden aus einer Triosonate Händels übernommen.

Nr. 10, d-moll, vielleicht das bedeutendste aller Orgelkonzerte Händels (Entstehungsjahr unbekannt), benützt im Finale das Presto aus der Klaviersuite in d-moll. Der dritte Satz stammt vom Herausgeber.

Nr. 11, g-moll, am 3. Januar 1750 beendigt, enthält als zweiten Satz eine Chaconne, der dritte ist mit leichten Veränderungen aus dem dritten Orgelkonzert (op. 4, Nr. 3) herübergenommen worden; das Larghetto (nach dem ersten Satz) stammt aus einer Kammersonate.

Nr. 12, B-dur (das fünfte Orgelkonzert Händels in dieser Tonart!), kurz nach 1740 entstanden (Chrysander), besteht nur aus zwei Sätzen, zwischen die der Herausgeber eine Sarabande aus einer Oboensonate Händels eingeschoben hat.

Der Organist von heute wird neben den großen, bedeutenden Konzerten in B-dur (Nr. 7), A-dur (Nr. 8) und d-moll (Nr. 10) auch in den seltener gespielten Konzerten Nr. 9, 11 und 12 Einzelsätze finden, mit denen er sich und seine Hörer erfreuen kann. Wir müssen uns nur vom Blick auf Bach ganz frei machen, wenn wir den Zugang zu dieser urgesunden, ungebrochenen, auch im Schmerz nie weichlichen Musik finden wollen.

Stuttgart, Herbst 1956   Hermann Keller

PREFACE

The good reception accorded to the first six Handel Organ Concertos in the present editor's arrangement for organ solo, encouraged the publishers to follow them with Concertos Nos. 7 – 12 (Handel's Op. 7, Nos. 1 – 6). The basis of the edition is the same; the orchestral portion is generally allotted to the Great (HW) and the solo part to the Swell (OW). The passages within a movement marked *ad libitum*, which Handel extended by improvisation when he himself played these concertos, have been supplemented by the editor; where complete movements are marked *ad libitum*, they have been borrowed from other Handel works. The tempo markings are original and also dynamic signs printed in large type; the editor's additions are shown in small type.

After the first six Handel Organ Concertos, published in 1738, which immediately enjoyed great popularity in concert and in private performance, six further concertos appeared in 1739/40, which, however, were not original works, but transcriptions from the Concerti Grossi. It is not certain whether Handel was generally concerned in this edition. Not until after his death, in 1760, did a further six original organ concertos appear as Op. 7, which dated from the period 1740 to 1751.

In particular it should be noted of these concertos: No. 7 (Op. 7, No. 1) is an exception to Handel's organ concertos inasmuch as it expressly demands two manual and pedals; a reed solo stop (Basson) on the manual is also required. Handel completed it on February 17, 1740; for which organ it was intended is not known. The first two movements are both in Chaconne form. The contrast in registration between Great and Swell must be particularly distinct for the purpose of expression.

No. 8 (Op. 7, No. 2), completed on February 5, 1743 in London, is in A major and commences with a fully developed French overture. The intermediary Adagio between the two Allegro movements is taken from a Handel Trio Sonata.

No. 9 (Op. 7, No. 3) in B flat, was commenced in 1741, but not completed until 1751. The main theme of the first movement is reminiscent of the 'Hallelujah' from 'Messiah'. Handel offers a choice of two Minuets for the final movement. An Adagio and Fugue should be improvised between the first and second movements; they have been transcribed from a Handel Trio Sonata.

No. 10, in D minor, perhaps the most important of all Handel's organ concertos (year of composition unknown), makes use in the Finale of the Presto from the Piano Suite in D minor. The third movement is by the editor.

No. 11, in G minor, completed on January 3, 1750, contains a Chaconne as its second movement; the third, with slight alterations, was taken by Handel from the third organ concerto (Op. 4, No. 3); the Larghetto following the first movement comes from a Chamber Sonata.

No. 12, in B flat (the fifth Handel organ concerto in this key!), dating from shortly after 1740 (Chrysander), consists of two movements only, between which the editor has inserted a Sarabande from a Handel Oboe Sonata.

In addition to the larger, more important concertos in B flat (No. 7), A major (No. 8) and D minor (No. 10), the present-day organist will find in the seldom-played Nos. 9, 11 and 12, single movements which will delight the player and his audience. We must free ourselves of the Bach outlook, if we would discover the approach to this original, cheerful, but never weakly-sentimental music.

Stuttgart, Autumn, 1954.

HERMANN KELLER
(English translation by Laurence Swinyard)

CONCERTO I
(B dur)

Georg Friedrich Händel op. 7 Nr. 1

OW.
f
HW. f
OW. mf
p HW.
p
OW. f
3 3
3
HW. p

f OW.
p HW.
tr
f OW.
f
(tr)
(tr)
p HW.
p
OW.   HW.   OW.
(HW.)
f

Bassons (Zungen)
HW.
OW.
HW.
f OW.
più f
(- Bassons)
+ Bassons
ff
tr
OW. mf
HW.
tr
tr
mf
tr

(Oboen)
OW.
HW.
p OW.
tr
HW.
OW. f
f

p
f
(ad libitum . . . . -)
più f
f
HW. f
OW.
HW.
f
OW.
HW.
p OW.
HW. p
f
OW.
HW. f
OW.
piano e adagio
p
p
1) oder

Andante
OW. p
f HW.
f
tr
p OW.
p
HW. p

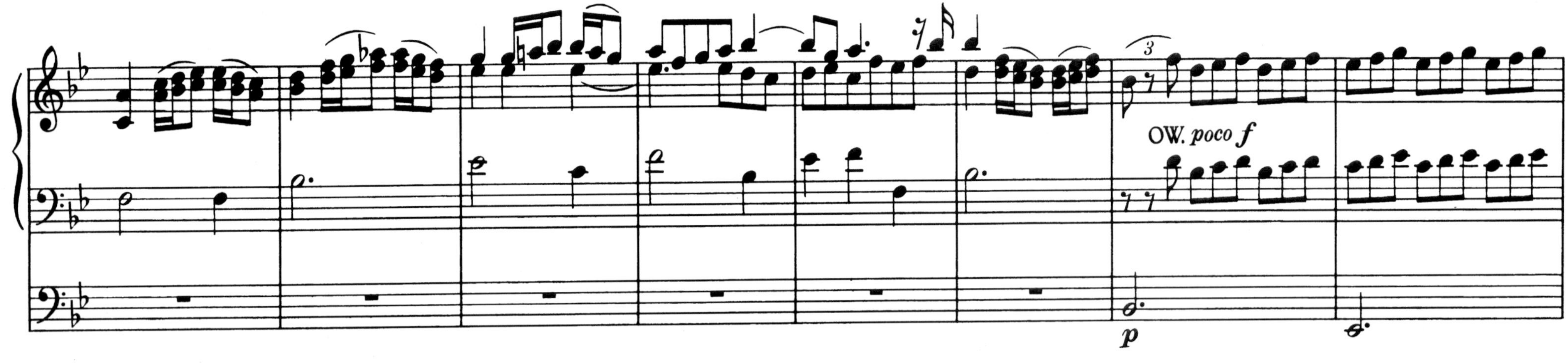
OW. poco f
p

HW. p

OW.
poco f
p (HW.)
HW.
f
(OW.)
f

OW.
p
pp
HW.
p
(OW.) p
OW.
p HW.
pp

1) „Organo a 2 Clav. e Pedale" schreibt Händel hier vor.

HW.
OW.
OW.
mf
tr
tr
tr
tr

più f
tr
f
HW.
f
Adagio
(tr)
p
p
p

Largo e piano
HW.
molto p
(mit 16')
tr

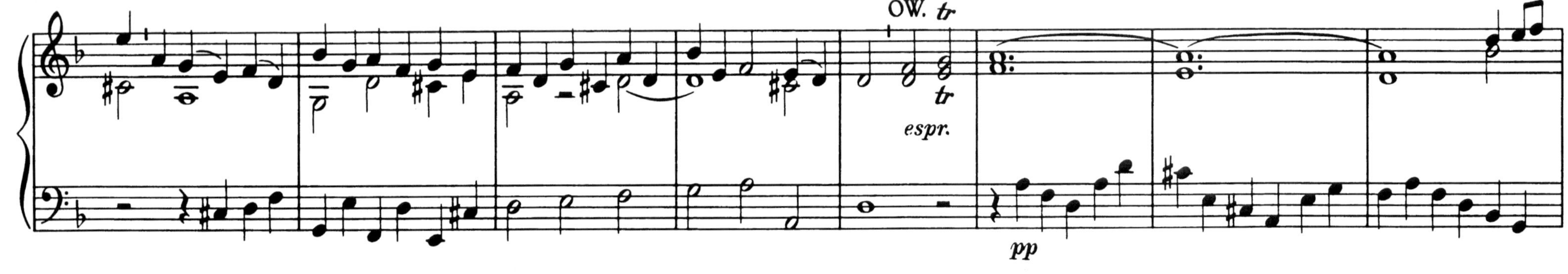

OW. tr
tr
espr.
pp

(tr)
(tr)
tr
HW. pp
pp
p

OW.
(tr)
(+16') HW.
(tr)
(tr)
HW.
pp

Bourrée

Allegro

HW. f

OW.
HW. p
p OW.
HW. p
p OW.
HW. p
f HW.
OW.

f HW.
OW.
HW.
ff (breiter)

CONCERTO II
(A dur)

Georg Friedrich Händel op. 7 Nr. 2

tr
tr
tr
f
HW.
(tr)
f (Org. Pl.)
tr

3
1.
2.

A tempo ordinario
HW.
mf
(mit 16')
tr
(8')
mf

più f
f
f

(Organo ad libitum)
ff
OW. f
tr
p
f
p
f
tr
f
tr
tr
tr
tr
tr
tr
tr
tr
tr
tr
tr

HW. f
(mit 16')
OW. f
p
f
più f

tr
HW. f
(Organo
OW. f
p dolce
OW.
ad lib.
mf

ff
f HW.
(mit 16′)
ff (etwas breiter)

(tr)
(tr)
Breiter

(Adagio)
(tr)

1) Original: ![tr.] etc.

OW. mp
OW.
mp mit 8'

HW.
f
(16')

OW.
3

HW.
HW.
(16')
1.
2.
OW. p
OW.
p (8' + 4')

HW. f
f
(16')
(tr)
OW. p
p (8')
tr
(tr)

HW.
f
HW.
OW.
p
OW.
p (8'+4')
dolce
HW. f
OW.
1. (tr)
p
2. tr

CONCERTO III
(B dur)

Georg Friedrich Händel op. 7 Nr. 3

HW.
p
p
tr
f
f
OW.
f
mf
tr
tr
3

HW. f
OW. p
HW. p
OW. mf
tr
f
f
p
tr
HW. p
f
OW. p
HW. p
OW.
HW.

OW.
HW.
OW.
con grazia
p
HW.
OW.
tr.
HW. f
f

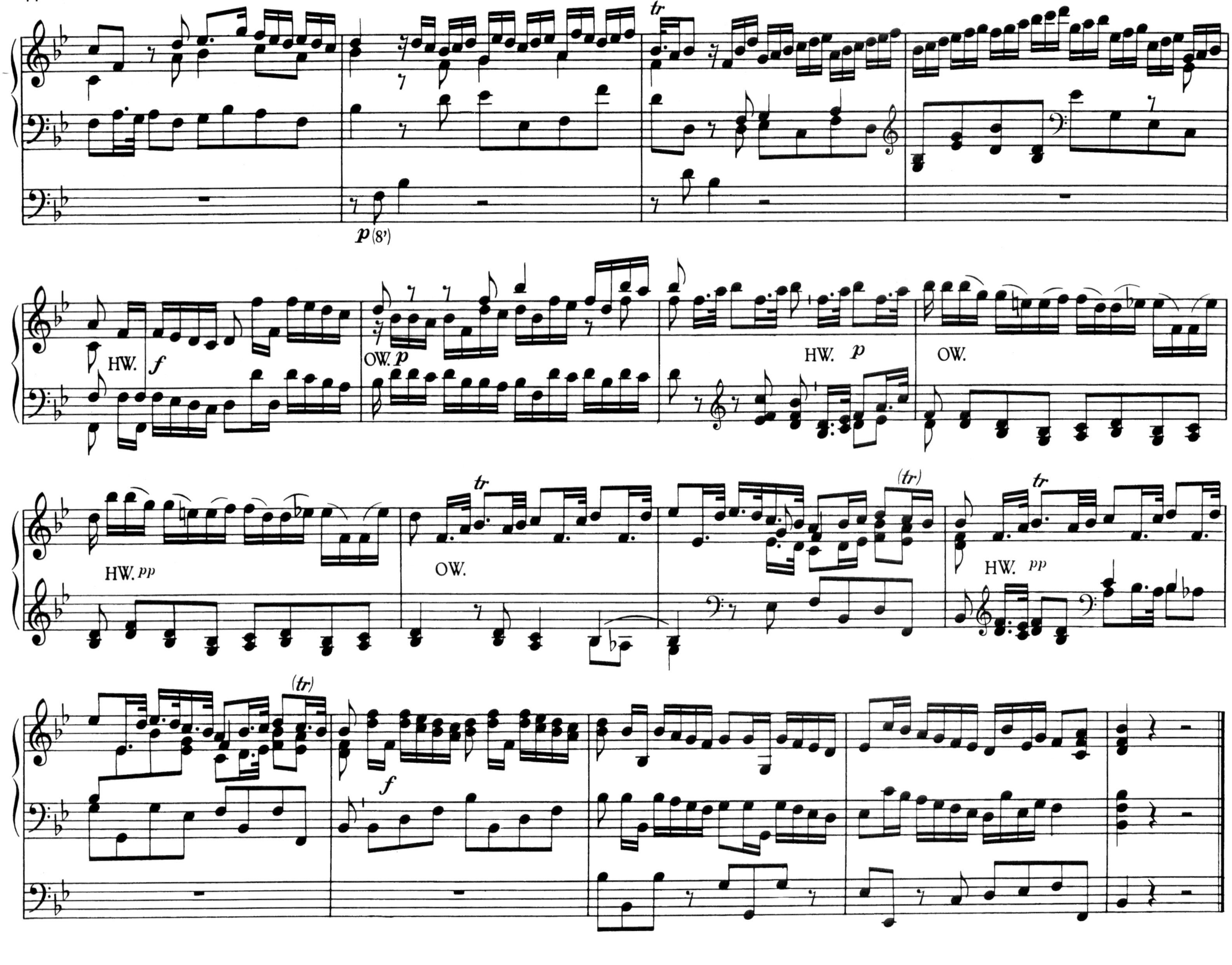

tr
p (8')
HW. f
OW. p
HW. p
OW.
HW. pp
OW.
(tr)
HW. pp
tr
(tr)
f

Adagio (Organo, Adagio e Fuga, ad libitum)
Alla breve
p
p

più f
Adagio
piano
piano

Spiritoso
HW. f
(tr)
(tr)
p
mf
f
OW.
mf
OW.
tr

HW.
p
HW. p
tr
OW.
(tr)
OW.
HW.
f
OW.
HW. pp
OW. p
HW. pp
OW.
mf
HW. pp
OW.
HW. p
OW. (pp)
HW. f
HW. p
pp
p
mf

f
OW.
HW.f

mf

OW.
p
pp HW.
(16') pianissimo e sostenuto

HW.
p tenuto

OW. f
p
f
HW. f
Adagio
tr
p
f
p
f
p

Menuett

p.
HW.
p
Breiter
f
f

Statt des vorhergehenden kann auch das folgende Menuett gespielt werden

Menuett

1) Original:    2) Wiederholung auf OW.

CONCERTO IV
(d - moll)

Georg Friedrich Händel op. 7 Nr. 4

OW.
mf espr.
p
(8')
(16')
HW.
tr
HW.
OW.
p
OW.
poco f
1) Original:
1) Original:

HW.
p
mf
(ad lib.)
tr
tr
f
OW.

tr.
tr.
tr.
3
tr.
HW.
ff
ff
ff
tr.
p

Allegro
OW. f
HW. f
p
f
3
f
f

OW. mf
pp
f
(ad lib. - - - - - - - - - - - -)
p
3

3
HW.
f
HW.
OW.
f
mf
pp
(ad lib. -

OW.
HW. f
(ad lib.
pp
(ad lib.
p
HW. f

(ad lib. arpeggiando
OW.
p
(ad lib. arp.

HW. f
p
f
p
3
f
più f
(etwas breiter)
f

Larghetto (Organo ad libitum)
p
p
pp

Allegro
tr
tr
HW. f
OW. mf
HW. f
(tr)
(tr)

OW. mf
p
tr
HW. f
tr
OW.

(tr)
HW. f
OW. f
più f
ff
ff
HW.
tr
tr
f
Breit

CONCERTO V

(g-moll)

Georg Friedrich Händel op. 7 Nr. 5

Allegro, ma non troppo, e staccato

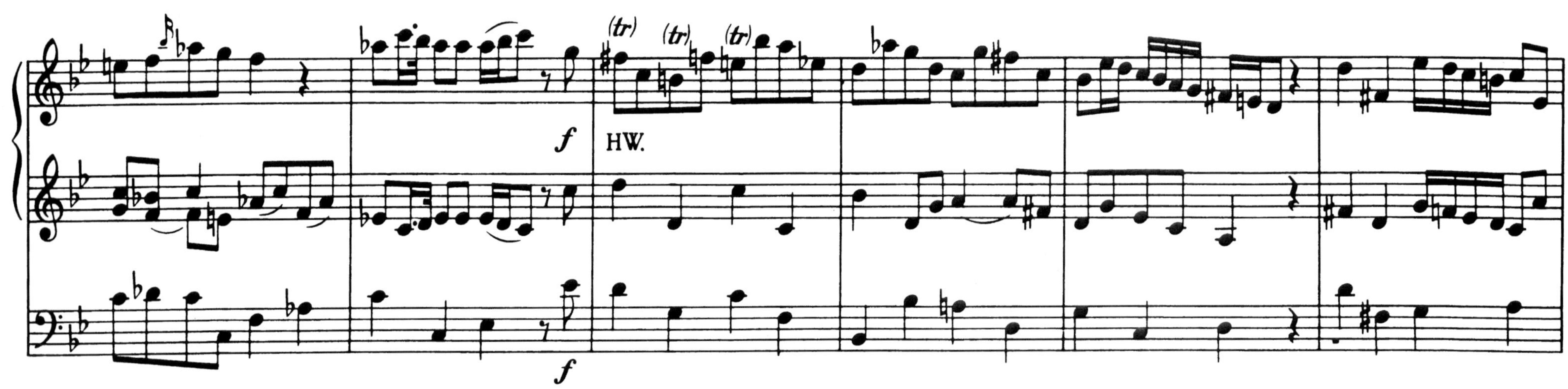

OW. p
f HW.
OW. p
HW. f
OW. p
tr
HW. f
OW. p
tr

HW. p
OW.
(tr)
HW. pp
pp
f
f
OW. p

HW. p
pp
OW.
p
p
pp
ad libitum
piu p, dolce
HW. f
(tr)

1) staccato = portato

1) Werden die Wiederholungen ausgeführt, so wechsle man die Manuale

mf
f HW.
tr
tr
1)
mf
p
p
p
p
1)

mf
mf
OW. f
f HW.
(l'ultima volta forte)

1) Die Wiederholung mit Manualwechsel

Gavotte
p
p OW.
tr

tr
f HW.
tr
OW.
tr
tr
HW. mf
OW.
tr

HW.
mf
tr
p OW.
(tr)
tr
HW. p
tr
p

CONCERTO VI
(B-dur)

Georg Friedrich Händel op. 7 Nr. 6

1) ♪♪. : das Sechzehntel etwas dehnen

HW. f
OW.
p

1) Original:

OW.
HW.
HW.
f
f
un poco piano
OW.
OW.

HW. f
f
OW.

HW. f
mf
p
Adagio

Larghetto *(Organo ad libitum)*

A tempo ordinario
HW. f
tr
f
f
tr
f

(ad libitum
tr
OW. mf
HW.
f
(ad libitum
OW. mf
f HW.
f

tr
f
tr
ad li-
OW. mf
bitum.
HW.
f
f
tr
tr
Fine